Dwelling in the Twilight Realm

Also by Don Langford

In the Light of the Full Moon: Dispersions, Glimpses, and Reflections

Songs from Deep Time

Dwelling in the Twilight Realm

Poems by

Don Langford

Published by D S Langford Publishing
Columbus, OH 43229
https://dslangfordpublishing.com

Printed in the United States

Cover Art Montage by Don Langford, 2023

Names: Langford, Don, author
Title: *Dwelling in the Twilight Realm* / Don Langford

ISBN 979-8-9867546-5-9 (pbk)
ISBN 979-8-9867546-6-6 (eBook)

Library of Congress Control Number: 2024901324

First Printing, February 2024

For Marlene, always inspiring

I believe in the future resolution of these two states, dream and reality, which are seemingly so contradictory, into a kind of absolute reality, a surreality, if one may so speak. It is in quest of this surreality that I am going, certain not to find it, but too unmindful of my death not to calculate to some slight degree the joys of its possession.

Andre Breton, *Manifesto of Surrealism*, 1924

The logic of dreams is superior to the one we exercise while awake. In dreams the mind at last finds its courage: it dares what we do not dare.

Etel Adnan, *Journey to Mount Tamalpais*, 1986

I sit quietly, listening to the falling leaves—
A lonely hut, a life of renunciation.
The past has faded, things are no longer remembered.
My sleeve is wet with tears.

Ryokan (1758-1831), from *One Robe, One Bowl*, translated by John Stevens, 1977

Contents

Part 1: Dreamscapes

Part II: Twilight Messengers

Part III: Toward the Waking State

About the Author   103

Part I: Dreamscapes

Asleep on the Shoreline

She held her webbed hand before my eyes
　　　　and said, "Do you believe me now?"

It happened inexplicably, without intent.
At the nape, when she swept her hair aside,
I clearly saw a pulsating set of gills
　　　　or a fluttering corrugated ventilator shaft
　　　　maybe it was a UPC code
　　　　misjudged in the glaring sunlight.

Disbelief turned to doubt.
Maybe it was the work of a tattoo artist
or some elective surgery,
but it moved and she was looking more reptilian
　　　　each time we met.

On later occasions she insisted that we meet by the sea
　　　　and she displayed scales on her arms and back,
　　　　overlapping and triangular, prehistoric.
　　　　"Feel," she said, taking my fingers
　　　　and pressing them to the cool hardness
　　　　where months earlier her soft velvety skin
　　　　　　had been sensual, soft, inviting.

Then she filed her teeth into sharp pointed biters
　　　　making her mouth look shark-like when she smiled.

Something began to change in her voice
　　　　a watery gurgle inviting me
　　　　to join her next time in the tide pool
　　　　　　then out beyond the breakwater
　　　　　　for deeper sea lessons.

When we kissed under water she breathed sweetness
        into my drowning lungs
        and pulled me down into depths
                where my eyes bulged and protruded
                and ears exploded into purple pulsations.

She left me breathless on the sandy seashore,
        watching and caring for me from her safe distance
        bobbing in the water through the night.

I allowed her to carry me back into the sea each morning at high tide,
        her gentleness and hypnotic power over me
        guiding with each soft gesture what life could be like if I wished.

After a time I lay alone,
waterlogged and battered,
exhausted in a sandy cove
wondering if I had any choice
        in the direction I would go that day.

Neighborhood Dream Cafe

We were counseled to remain silent about the loss
of our memories or any confusions that lingered
about the atrocities we had witnessed.

This we learned from anonymous notes
strewn about the cafe we visit on our nightly rounds,
and lipstick reminders adorning the mirrors in our hotel room.

Some of the messages we may have posted ourselves;
others, like those pinned to walls
or carved into the wooden tables
and bar tops, were intended to
sow doubt and mistrust among the patrons.

Cryptic messages were folded
into our serviettes, strychnine droplets in the coffee,
even the waiters averted their eyes
when we used their threatening notes as currency
to pay our bills.

We know they laughed like hyenas in the cafe kitchen
after we exited with leftovers dripping in our pockets.
We'll see who laughs when they discover what happened
to the quarters in the jukebox or the peppermints on the counter.

We have grown distracted by pettiness
while there are snipers in the streets and in the courts
picking us off one by one like sleepwalkers in an arcade.

In our consolation we return again each evening
to the same neighborhood cafe
never knowing what to expect,
never knowing if we will remember
what we did the night before.

Another Day of the Dead

Festive afternoons of draped crepe paper
gave way to nightmarish evenings
where sleepwalkers in the cafe of lost dreams
pulled on the brims of their sombreros
beneath the white-boned skulls
decorating the darkened bar
on the Day of the Dead.

How is it not possible to know
that one is being haunted
by the glares from the coal-black eye sockets
shifting in the flickering light,
reminding the tequila drinkers
that their mothers and fathers
are patiently waiting in their graves
for something good to come
of the sons and daughters who abandoned them
in their late-life time of need?

The worm at the bottom, the hooked bait,
works its way into the skulls leaning against
the booth backs and brass bar rails,
eating from the inside the catch of the day.
The boisterous jesting, the happy backslapping,
and the early evening furtive eye gazing
turn to quiet somber catatonia
hours after the haunting inner voices
rise out from under the volcano,
and large insects crawl along the inner eyelids
where no one else sees them.

Soon they are walking along the bar top,
and across the mirror and walls,
large crusty-shelled and noisy, their staccato feet tapping

faster and louder, and the faces of the people at the bar look on accusingly
and yet oblivious to the clattering noise of the armadillo bugs
dodging behind the liquor bottles into the damp and darkened corners.

Elbows on the bar top, hands pressing tightly against the ears,
one and two, and then three grown men try to keep out the cries
of loved ones abandoned, helpless figures lying on the roadside,
reaching out their hands in a final pleading gesture.
Then the soft sobbing begins and the bartender looks at his watch;
still two hours before closing time and sending the day's catch
into the night where they will find a way to wipe away
guilt and loneliness until the gnawing brings them back again
for more. They will not remember the brief glimpses they had
of something rotting deep inside. The vagueness will be transformed
by the next afternoon into a need for camaraderie.

The faint smell of bleach, the mopped floors, the glossy bar top
welcome the return of the dwellers of forgotten nightmares,
and no one remembers the armadillo cockroaches crawling over their hands
and into their shirt sleeves. There's news and gossip to bring the patrons
together yet again, sipping the first round that, this time, may take them
closer to euphoria or the land of a new rising sun.

One of the men rubs a wet finger round and round
in little circles on the bar top, pressing it like a coiling spring
almost hypnotically, as if he is pushing something through,
then he slowly swirls the last mouthful at the bottom of his glass
and asks the bartender for another.

Wormwood Memories

I remember saying to her, when I could no longer see
my fingers or back of hand,
"I have never reached this far inside of a wound."
With a soft smile or grimace, she drifted—her eyes rolling back,
seeking islands of calm, clouds to drift on.

Deep inside, I removed tangles of string and knotted wire,
burnt brush, and the debris of centuries of war, conflict, feuds.

"Don't leave me," came her whisper, a sigh,
a kind of gurgle from under water, a hissing in my ear.

Transatlantic missives, SOS wires, Teletype codes,
        for years a correspondence of fragments,
        pieces of wartime conversation, encoded
                so today I can only guess their meaning:

"Skated today on the pond," she wrote. "Saw Basho's frog, plop!"
What to do with such fragments carried in my pocket.

"The canyons are yawning in the thunder"— This once meant something to
me; I'm sure of it.

"No squirrels to eat the tulip bulbs this winter"— I can't unravel this,
no matter how many times I replay it through the darkened nights
        without her.

Long ago in summertime, at a small paint-flecked wooden table
near the wild plum tree, we tasted Retsina, Ouzo, and Wormwood,
        in hot dry wind—

        We called the Santa Ana the Mistral,
        marooned romantics in the California sun.

A Surrealist Account of a Silent Zen Buddhist Retreat

Sleeveless robes, windswept and soaked in rose-petal dew
        hung without smiles on minstrel's pegs
        high in the fog-tipped mountains
        waiting for an entry

Heraldic cherubs, robed ticket-takers
        shave-pates, beaming through young amethyst eyes
        groomed in baldness like silenced parrots;

        adorning the rainy hillsides, the sound of
        one-handed thunder clapping,
        but who hears the storm?

In the back row a monk whips an ox cart,
        another pours tea, overflowing the guests' cups,
        and a third holds a flower stem waiting for the right no-words

Under a wind-rippled canopy outside, a band tunes instruments
        not knowing yet that they have been invited to the wrong address
        for their afternoon recital.

        Peacocks wander the hillsides,
        trumpeting marauders squawking at the rest notes
                in their own musical score

The recitation is about to begin; everyone extinguishes their ideas and
        thought bubbles, waiting for a Cage at the piano
        or radiant Buddha on a pillow

Thinking of not thinking, the guests uncross their legs
        in pained restlessness,
        when will authority intervene, answer all the questions,
        and begin the mime show?

Is it appropriate to break into uproarious applause?
Do I dare to laugh, guffaw, or eat a peach?

Over in the glen, the band gauges the monkish mood
  and begins to play the opening notes of Bach's
  improvisational fugue for bagpipes and didgeridoo

There seems to be something amiss, the crowd is stirring;
  the raised perfumed dais is now a coy pond;
  the trapeze performers and hunger artists
  have folded their carrying cases and headed for the hills

No business cards offering discounted hip replacements, lube jobs,
  or precision arthroscopic chakra alignments.

Everyone is ushered outside, invited to recline
  in the clover-blossomed grass.

All the confiscated phones are buzzing in a box
  at the end of the long driveway
  as the first shrieks of anxiety and loss are let loose, cascading into
  a chorus of sorrowful coyote yelping among the visitors
  tormented into forced silence and wide-eyed wonder.

Soon some are moaning, others om like a groan from
  the seventh ring. Some offered consolation and solace
  to one another,
  others dig deep pits in the lawn with their bare hands,
  in the event that nerve gas is released;
  those who plugged their ears sobbed the loudest,
  rocking back and forth in their half-lotus meltdown.

Interviewed later, some followers reported staring hypnotically
  at the peacocks who pranced in step with the thrumming

of bagpipes and didgeridoos, then standing and whirling
dervishly like dizzy spinning tops until they were swept
into a love-lunge with the wet hillside grasses.

Others spoke of being transported into clove-scented chambers,
old milk-wagons from their childhood, or age-regressed
into earlier lives when they washed laundry
on the Ganges and went swimming at Sils Maria.

Others were certain that the Buddha rose out of the coy pond
and delivered a sermon that is already available
in the bookstores, more powerful than anything they
had ever heard, using up every cell of their mental powers,
leaving no room in their memory to recall what had been said.

Others saw through the charade, the hallucination, the illusory
pandemonium to the truth that lay behind
all the stage maneuvers.

It was a 4-dimensional jeweled sermon seen from the angles
of all who were there; a multi-faceted beam of light guided
through the prisms of the individual dewdrops of consciousness
that settled together in that space where beliefs and cynicisms
were melted into an alloy that would adhere to every vibrating
cell in their bodies.

The bumper-sticker mantra became "An understanding beyond knowing."

And they knew when they returned home, no one would believe them,
so they would have to admit that nothing special happened:
some peacocks sang to the bagpipes and a coy pond glistened
after the rain.

Composting the World

First, we composted the leaves
      collected from gutters

            tossed in coffee grounds and lettuce leaves
            tore up the avocado skins and crushed the egg shells

            and the garden grew

In time, we added furniture, especially wooden legs
      and electrical light fixtures

            we found ceramic toilet bowls and old urinals
            and concrete blocks from construction sites

            Adding crunch to the growing pile we needed moisture
            so the city's sewage water was sprayed on the growing heap
            using timed geysers commissioned by the garden club

            We found abandoned elevator shafts that we tossed
                  on the pile at odd angles

Someone donated old teletype machines
and farm implements—combines and tractors were stacked high

an airplane and millions of gallons of jet fuel helped to bring heat
      to the growing pile

A uranium mine was trucked in from across the country,
then an aquarium, and not to be outdone,
a decommissioned military base
was transported with fanfare, parades, and marching bands

Meteorologists worked hard to bring in a tornado from Oklahoma,
        guiding it carefully with satellites

The flow of major rivers was redirected to moisten the pile

volunteers from across the country worked day and night
in a real national effort

and before long it was a global project; all the wars were halted,
diseases ceased, and violence redirected
into the global composting effort

It seemed as if all of our problems were finally solved
once we committed ourselves to sharing our ingenuity and talent.

Lost in the Observatory

Looking through the telescope an eye blinked back at me;
it happened only once; first I thought it was my own eye
so I blindfolded both eyes and tried it again.

I had to report later
        that it was then that someone
        must have stolen the telescope.

It had been there only a moment before
        while I was binding the kerchief
        around my head and over my eyes.

The arresting officer took me in for questioning
        I demanded to know if I was being charged
        with a crime:

Theft of a telescope, public property
        lying to an officer
        tampering with evidence
        leaving the scene of a crime
        failure to offer assistance to an ailing officer
        jay walking
                jay walking!
        underage smuggling

But I'm an old man, I insisted;
a blind old man looking for the stars.
Any constellation will do.

Maybe I was dropped off here by mistake
a blind cat expected to find its way home.

"Put him in the pen," someone said.
"Let him sleep it off."

Going All the Way Back

At first, the saline solutions
took me back to the coastal tidepools
iridescent green anemones
        slippery rocks
        the briny beginnings

There were some conversations
and reports about age regression
before we increased the dosage
        that took us into deep time

Several surgeries before the lungs
could accept the constant flow
of ocean water, filtering out the sand

Slowly we acquired the taste of kelp,
eating one ribbon at a time,
learning to stay down below
        and see without squinting
        in the calm coolness beneath the waves

The changes were at first gradual,
then the markings of time
dissolved in this new home
of gurgling bubbles
        and droning undertones—
        a life in aqueous filtered light

Movement graceful,
        suspended in amniotic sea gel
        reckoning with ancient neighbors
        who teach by doing

And still some older urge to shed complexity
　　　to explore earlier forms
　　　　　to be resting in the sun
　　　　　and wind and spiraling gases
　　　　　bumping into other elements
　　　　　with affinities and repulsions
　　　　　　guiding every movement

Mayfly Karma Dream

I must have realized that I had been complaining too much
    about life and humanity
    when suddenly a dream-filled sleep overtook me

and in that state I found myself in the company
    of hundreds of others
    gathered around a pond

some of the people said
    they were bored with life
    and slept much of the time

many others described a life of running in circles,
    mouths agape,
    eating the world and everything in it.

At dusk we all succumbed to a sudden drowsiness
    as fog descended on the pond
    and our lives, we thought, were being forever changed

When the sun rose the following morning
    we were a swarm of mayflies
    buzzing frantically

What then concerned us, I recall,
    is that we had no mouths
    to voice our complaints

    and no digestive system
    to consume the world
    as we had been accustomed

and that by the end of day
we would all be dead
after our lifetime of 24 hours

Soon all the loud wailing and mouthless screams around the pond
were enough to wake me
from my dream

That morning I ate my oatmeal very quietly,
without complaint of the human realm, grateful
to be afforded another precious day
to see what this world of wonder had to offer

The Sleepwalker

Guided by the voice
she shuffled through the darkened house,
robe draped over bony frame,
opening the window blinds—and waiting.

Who is coming this time?
Who will not arrive this time
      before she returns
      to forgetful sleep?

Beguiled by the calm night voice, her trusted huckster,
      she is no Cassandra.
We take her back to bed
not awaiting news from the future—no glimpses or premonitions;
      only the hope that she will sleep.

Only we will remember, at daybreak,
that she stood, convinced,
      at the window
      peering into darkness
      with an urgency . . .
            that someone was coming to see her
            and she must be there to greet them.

For her, in daylight, this never happened.
At the breakfast table she has no recollection.
Maybe it is only for us to witness
until someday, when we hear our own night voices
      calling to us of some urgent need,
      we may believe that our delusions are insights
          or that the events never happened at all.

Early Morning Dream

From the drowsy recesses of memory
       a musty cardboard shoe box appears,
       free-floating at first
           in dreamlike space.

Inside, a jumble of faded postcards
       with green Canadian two-cent stamps affixed,
a grandmother's cursive hand, looping letters
       describing a visit to Montreal,
       its cobblestone roads, bright blue window boxes,
       white cascading cotoneasters in June,
           French-speaking school girls
           skipping home in their uniforms.

And then two or three undated postcards about the war,
the death of boys they knew
noted briefly in an unwavering hand, words without emotion
       accompanied by a small newspaper clipping

and that is it . . .
a life contained
in a brief passing reference
inside a shoe box
now only faintly remembered
years after it too has disappeared.

And a grandmother's tobacco-stained fingers
glimpsed in memory
before the smell of death
brought an end to a morning dream show.

The Ventriloquist

The curtain opened on the stage
and soft blue light fanned downward
on the two figures seated quietly on wooden stools,
their feet dangling several inches above the floor.

The two figures looked and dressed alike,
blue checkered shirts and dark puffy pants,
identical in every way except size;
the larger of the two sat on the left,
the much smaller on the right slumped with head down
until the act started.

They both had clownish faces, brightly painted,
crease marks at the mouth and chin, as if hinged,
so that when they spoke their mouths opened
up and down in exaggerated vertical lines.

Their bright wide eyes winked and rolled
like cartoon figures when they expressed feelings
as they spoke. In this, too, they appeared identical.

A large sleeved arm extended behind the two figures
joining ventriloquist and dummy.
Soon the large figure on the left introduced the act
and thanked the audience for coming.

Turning to the dummy he began asking questions
and the dummy answered, moving its head from side to side,
turning its eyes for comic emphasis.

From the table between the two figures,
the ventriloquist picked up a glass of water, moving
mechanically exactly as the dummy moved.
He drank from the glass as the dummy described

21

what it was like growing up as a dummy,
always on the road, sleeping in a suitcase,
folded flat with his feet in his face.

The ventriloquist played a harmonica, smoked
a cigarette, and counted from one to ten
all while the dummy recounted what it was like
always playing second fiddle and not getting
his fare share of the earnings.

The audience members laughed at the comical parts
and applauded the challenging and skillful parts
of the act. The skit lasted ten to fifteen minutes and,
as usual with such acts, it came to its conclusion
with the ventriloquist asking the dummy to thank the audience
and say good night.

And as the crowd applauded politely,
the dummy stepped down from the stool and bowed
as the ventriloquist slumped
into a small pile on the stool
and a loud gasp of incredulity filled the room.

Many in the audience were still shaking their heads
as they walked out of the theatre into the rainy streets,
sometimes looking twice at their companion
or at their own hands for some sign of certainty,
some even fearful that the rain would remove
the paint from their faces.

A Night at the Nobby Nob

In the pointillist style
we saw the patrons up close
as large dots in our vision;
      we couldn't help it.

Only when we drew back
far enough to fold our arms
without touching the others
      did we see them clearly
      for what they were

We recounted the Scotch broom
on the hillsides by the sea
fragrance deepening

the pungent lawn violets
crushed underfoot

lachrymose eye ducts
open for want of tears
before an obedient mirror

the spines of books
cracking and twisting,
their vertebrae folding inward

and all the occasions
made for loud and longing laughter
uprooted from fondness

scorching the keyboards
of pianos wheeled into the courtyard,
chandeliers ablaze with amethyst
      glass teardrops

dancers flung their skirts high
through the swirls of night sky,
uneven cobblestones glistening in the rain

even the lone drinkers
in the darkened corners
bolted their blinkers to the stage

waiting for marionettes to appear
amid the puffs of smoke
to turn the midnight dreams
into confetti floating above the rooftops

and in the closeness of embraces
sought for in the anonymous darkness
even a kiss will do before leaving

a thunderclap snapped people to attention,
some rose to forgive themselves
and others turned white as ghosts

only a cistern could carry the tears
wept before the open flames of dawn
too late to get home early

some held their hands outward
fingertips touching to say goodbye,
skirts and zippers stowed
           for the long walk to purgatory

Lesson for Day One

Hot summer day, parched dry beach
a single wooden stand in the distance
palm fronds draped over the roof
bananas stacked high beside a row of blenders
large sign reading "LEMONADE 25 ¢"

I ask the old toothless man for one lemonade,
wiping my brow in anticipation,
setting down a quarter.

Minutes later he places before me a paper plate
and on it a brown pile of banana mash
and a plastic spoon

I look up to see the old man disappear
behind a cloth curtain

At a nearby table I eat my banana mash;
other people arrive and place their orders.

When I have finished eating
I dispose the paper plate and spoon
and return to the wooden shack

I say to the old man that I had ordered a lemonade.
He looked deeply into my eyes
as a loving teacher might to a favored pupil, and said,
"Wha you espeh from banana?"

Dream State Beside a Pond

Inside the dream
a landslide of signs and symbols

translate these
beneath the suffocating rubble

lying there
hearing only vibration and hum

a courtyard of words
evaporating in the sun

long ago
toboggan rides on icy hills
gliding home

today mid-morning pond sounds
lotus pods popping
in yellow fans of sunlight

Fragrant grasses call me back
hillside meadow
blue sky, patchy fog
all embracing

Dream Dialogue in Five Voices

Man 1: Just like a solipsist.

Man 2: What did you say?

Woman 1: He said you're talking like a solipsist.

Woman 2: [whispering]: What's a solipsist?

Man 2: I'm not the only one here, you know, who's a little troubled by our predicament.

Woman 1: [whispering]: It's someone who thinks they're the only one in the world . . .

Woman 2: [whispering]: How is that even possible?

Woman 3: I've heard that if we remain calm and quiet, things will come to us.

Woman 2: What kind of things?

Woman 3: Oh, you know. Important things. Answers.

Woman 2: What kind of answers can you get if you're just quiet?

Man 2: What I'd like to know is how we got into this mess in the first place.

Woman 1: We've been having a little side conversation over here. And we came to . . . the conclusion . . .

Man 2: You mean you haven't even been listening?

Man 1: I think it was Dostoevsky, wasn't it, who said in order to escape from prison you first have to . . .

Woman 3: Listen everyone, I have an idea. Let's sit in a little circle. No, really.

Woman 1: This is very similar to how we worked it out last time. Do you remember? Okay, let's summarize: Some of us were feeling a little frustrated. Remember?

Man 1: "Bedraggled," I think was the word we used.

Woman 1: Yes, bedraggled, like Willy Loman.

Man 1: That's right, That's riiiight. Remember Willy telling Biff to get his valise.

Woman 1: Don't forget the infidelity?

Man 2: And he said, "Biff, I'm giving you an orda"

Man 1: Yes, "That's an oarda"

All: "That's an orda. I'm giving you an orda."

Man 2: "Someday you'll grow up and understand. These things happen. They don't meeean anything."

Woman 1: That was the key point. The problem in a nutshell. It was the question of meaning.

Man 1: We were talking . . .

Woman 3: about the love we all could share?

Man 1: No. About where meaning resides. Remember the example: Suppose you got a letter from your grandmother when you were a child.

Woman 1: Yes, and years later, after she has died, you reread that letter. It's the same letter; the same words on the same page.

Man 2: And we asked ourselves, "Does the letter take on a different meaning later?"

Man 1: And it does.

Woman 1: It most certainly does.

Man 1: And that leads to the question, "Where does meaning reside?"

Woman 2: And what was the answer to that question?

Woman 3: I think if we sit quiet and still the answer will come to us.

Woman 1: We agreed that the meaning doesn't reside in the letter . . .

Man 2: Or in the person reading the letter.

Woman 1: We came to the conclusion that meaning is fluid

Man 1: More a verb than a noun, right?

Man 2: It's an interaction between the reader and the text.

Woman 1: That's the point we need to keep in mind throughout . . .

Man 1: It's important

Woman 2: But difficult

Woman 1: To stay focused.

Woman 3: My meditation class talks about this a lot.

Man 1: Who remembers *My Dinner with Andre*?

Woman 3: We have these deep discussions, then we feel good about ourselves.

Woman 1: And what about meaning? What's the point of it.

Woman 3: Then we sit quietly and have our own experiences.

Man 1: Just like a solipsist.

Man 2: What did you say?

Part II: Twilight Messengers

Ways to Say Goodbye

Drop all the petals at once
windblown end of season
         winter chill setting in
         the once vibrant colors
         no longer holding on
         letting go in a moment

A carefully written note
         held in place on the table
         with a token thank-you gift
         hinting of a later return
         —a jar of jam or sprig of mint—
         in early morning while everyone sleeps

Place a half-filled satchel by the door
         like a guest waiting for check-out time
         let the days ripen with conversation,
         slowly adding to the bulging pack,
         warm embraces before departure

Find a quiet place to lay down the bones
         like Jeffers' deer
         in sunny outcropping
         overlooking the sea,
         waves chanting in the background

Over the Edge

At the edge of sleep on your own,
      leaning out over the abyss
      night after night,
      cremnophobia has invaded
      even the spaces
      where once you closed your
      eyes to the fears
          and the treatments
          that took you to the edges
             of rooftops.

You sat blindfolded
on bridges over rivers,
      feeling the metal girders,
      hearing the flowing water below
      pulling you to your knees
          whimpering, babylike
          crying for solace.

In the canyon hikes
the guides walked on,
      leaving you clinging
      to a spindly tree trunk
      like an imploring lover
          panting on the overhang,
          "Do not leave me here alone."

And now you sit at the top of the carpeted stairs
      wide-eyed octogenarian
      after a lifetime of accomplishments
      calling out to an empty world,
      "Is there anyone down there
      who can help me?
      I'm about to fall again."

Protecting the Little Turtles

In the last dream
before dreaming ceased
     in endless sleeplessness

there was a line of tiny turtles
     crossing the road
and we joined the people
who were lifting or escorting them
to safety in the sandy coastal dunes
where they would lay their eggs

Cars raced by, honking horns
     and crushing dozens of turtles
     heedless of the efforts to save the slow-paced creatures

In the dream some of the people carried turtles to their safety,
     then derailed cars from the roadway,
     watching them careen into fiery piles
     or explode over cliff sides into the waiting sea

With sneering smiles some abandoned the turtles altogether
     to focus their efforts on dismantling the traffic
     that raced fiercely through the turtle crossing.

Some of the turtle protectors ripped out the roadway signs
     warning traffic of sharp turns ahead
     and even posted new signs
     that directed traffic over the embankment
     into the foamy sea

Waking from this last dream to the news of new human atrocities
     and the cruelties one inflicts on the unknown others,
     each with his or her own family to protect and love,
        each with a simple desire for safety

Little Paper Boat

A little paper boat floated past me downstream
in my dream last night,
or it may have been a candle or a leaf;
something impermanent, a life perhaps
of someone dear, floating on into another place
        out of view.

It was more peaceful than I thought it would be—
a quiet soft gliding moment; a stillness
        full of peace.

Someone—a woman—dressed in white
sat cross-legged on the bank,
gazing to the other shore
while the little white boats, shaped like hats,
carried tiny candles on their winding way
        downstream.

There was calm patience
in the faces of other people who appeared
along the green grassy bank,
saying to me in slow quiet tones,
to accept the news that will arrive
in the coming days.

"She is dying peacefully," says the woman
dressed in white; "Let her go and she will send you news
when you need to hear it from downstream
where the willow trees overhang the rippling water."

In my dream the acceptance of her death
had the softness of those falling leaves
that come to rest on the moving current.

The last journey along the watercourse is silent,
and even for those watching from the banks
this is a kind of preparation.

The Eye at Nightfall

At any other time
we would have preferred to sleep
or seek a source for numbing the pain

But now we must awaken,
remain vigilant and persistent

The numbers of people have grown
the number of possible nightmares
          has magnified

The lid is coming down
          on a boiling pot

More of the neighbors are suffering
          more than we ever imagined
          and in ways we never saw before

The silent spreading famine
and the wounds of war,
once concealed and hidden from view,
are today brought before us to witness
so we can no longer feign ignorance
          or remain innocent, untouched

And among those who see opportunity in tragedy
some are already drawing up plans
          to herd the cattle into pens

                    and secure their own safety
                    behind fortified fences
                    and impenetrable walls

Daily life will bear some resemblance
>   to what it was yesterday
>   only to those who are dozing

To the others with eyes open,
>   one eye looks over a shoulder;
>   the other watches the collapse of a dream

The call goes out in the night
>   to rally the human spirit
>   as it has done before
>   in times before long darkness

Opening the Heart in Red Rock Canyon

You were reaching deep into the earth that day, pushing
up red hot fiery rock of living memory, describing your smothering
journey into blackness

>We moved slowly through the canyon
>that had thrown up red rock in early upheaval,
>reshaping itself, transforming the landscape
>into a jewel of light and life

You had moved beyond the reach of caring hearts
into the realm of the one-way dive
drinking the pitch black midnight
that boiled your brain and dried your desires for meaning

>We pulled into a turnout where you stood
>above the valley, smiling for a photo
>with cliffs behind you in the distance

You had pulled yourself down into the darkness
of the soul where loneliness feeds only on the company
of a self that has grown tired of moving on—
a world unhinged from any meaning,
nothing left but the letting go

>We looked at the landscape that had constantly renewed itself,
>juniper and barrel cactus healing the valley,
>sunlight warming the autumn earth

You had looked beyond the silver backing of the mirror
into the gulf beyond yourself, beyond any recognizable reflection,
and in that darkest death nudge where all desire and hope have vanished,
you washed your face and drank water, deep survival instinct awakening
out of the blackness beyond thought

We turned from one scenic overlook to another,
at times hearing only the sound of the breeze
blowing through dense desert brush that had learned
to survive on the morning dew, then
we headed home

You had turned back to life, responding to the shiver in your brain,
the wordless summons to begin the long journey home.

Soft Fading Song

Everything will be provided for you
        the meals, friendships, heartbreaking news,
        the end of certainties

The rain and the music will vie
        for your wavering attention

In a coastal town long ago
        colloidal silver sea
        fog-filled morning,
        a palette of memories

Snapshots, fleeting glimmers in the mind,
        projected against the last standing walls
        encircling an enfeebled body
        lying awake after years of running,
        trying to press meaning out of the vastness of days

Then the thunder rumbles overhead
        bass sounds to the incessant rain drops
        pounding against the music inside

Attention glides on its own smooth path,
        asking where was that sandy cove,
        all the sailboats lined up?
        Why were we there?

And when there is no one to answer the questions,
        the fearful whispers in the night,
        or the sighs of giving in to the loss
        of another thought, another word,
            another little part
            of what was assembled in a life,

including the letting go of a self,
what then?

Who will care when the fog-filled mornings
say good night to the soft fading song
or the final sound of rain on the roof?

Unceremonious Darkness Falls

Half the nation are prophets,
half are sleepwalkers
on the march to catastrophe.

So many eyes in retreat
for lack of seeing.

Forests are being massacred
to make coffins
for the dead,
and the youngest saplings
sacrificed to make holiday toothpicks.

For those farthest from the source
the signal is weakest;
forests fall to those who are near
while laughter and mirth are faint echoes
of faraway death and brutality.

Out of ashes and silence
grows the resistance of reason
like the quiet planting
of new seedlings
in the dark and merciless ruins.

The Still and Changing Sea

In this crossover world
of shared borrowings
tall Ponderosa pines drop their heavy cones
next to glossy-leafed Magnolias
shiny in the morning sun,
and palms grow in fanned clusters
near clumps of desert oat grasses
that spread toward the sandy dunes
and the smooth white sands of Florida's Gulf Coast.

This is a quiet world in December,
a few strolling visitors on the beach,
here by some unknown invitation,
some walking barefoot along the shoreline
carrying their shoes in curled fingers.

There is still mystery in the breaking waves,
unending in their hypnotic rhythm
the changing stillness
in its coming and going;
here, we are looking back at our first home
past the long ebb and flow of tides and time,
past all the differences and changes
that brought us here.

Near these calm shores
seekers and plunderers sought their fountains of youth,
pillagers racing and raging through
the source of life at their feet
It is here at the shore's edge
that the youth-giving mist of the sea
touches the land in its long caress;
it is here that the earth renews itself.

This wide and never-ending expanse of the sea
speaks its own ancient language
for the patient sea-farer to decipher
and the shore-wandering visitors to feel
in the quiet incessant music of its call

What Do We Have to Say?

And for those of us
for whom calamity and catastrophe
have not touched our lives,
have we nothing to say
about the silent deaths in our family,
the usual kinds of malpractice in the hospital
or the neuropathies associated with alcohol
or the slow robbing of a mind by dementia?

These are the small individual earthquakes
that do not leave rubble in the streets.

These are the silent pains at the bedside
where there are no bombed out buildings
or bloodied bodies in the street.

We do not huddle with neighbors to share
        our grief and wailings.

We are alone with a father who is suffocating
        in a hospital room on Thanksgiving weekend
        when the part-time staff are laughing down the hall.

We are bent over a donated bed where a mother
        is sinking with her gray-skinned face
        into the last gurgling sleep,
        leaving us helpless at her bedside.

We are saying goodbye to a young sister
        who wears pink slippers on her painful feet
        saying to us don't worry, meaning she wants to go.

For those of us who grew up with the American Dream
        coming across the border from Canada,

living like the *Leave It to Beaver* family on TV,
uneventful immigrants like our forebears
from Ireland and Romania
who struggled in their own silent ways,
what do we have to say
in the quiet privilege we have fallen into?

We have no photographs or newspaper clippings
about devastation felt by thousands;
for that we marvel at our good fortune.

We are saddened by the catastrophes of nature
and the inhumanity of war
and the devastation that leaves millions
marked forever if they survive.

We watch quietly while we write our poems,
our imaginary escapes from something hidden,
little abstract wonderings, the aimless wanderings
of searching minds in the ephemeral clouds,
escaping from the end of the line,
driving in circles in a kind of orphaned freedom.

We have nothing to say except to create new echoes
that resound off the walls of our own experiences,
a tiny packet of papers for no one else to read;
just a few short volumes to say we, too, were here.

Key Chain Revelation

For a time we pulled out the yarrow stalks
consulted the I-Ching,
divining meaning from the ancient text.

We were certain that our chance meeting
with friends far from home
or the best course of action
in our lives
could be divined
if only we could read the signs,

like a locksmith or a thief listening
to the sound of tumblers falling into place,
revealing inside the safe
the long hidden treasure.

At the beach a week later
with our blankets spread,
sandwiches, grapes, and biscuits
neatly arranged,
a swift and stealthy seagull swooped,
lifting our shiny key chain
into the air fast along the coastline,
first over sand, then over shallow ocean waves,
leaving both of us, mouths agape, in disbelief.

And only much later
after retrieving the dampened keys
did we wonder what meaning
lay in that act of theft
coming from the clear sky above.

In a Quiet Moment

When she left
even for a short time
and the room was no quieter than
  when she had been here,
  it felt emptier, much emptier.

What begins as the faint murmurs
  of mortality,
  the sudden onset
  of a new condition or ailment,
  the longer bedridden days
  and more frequent hospitalizations,
  turns the heart inward
  the better to touch other hearts
  in some little way.

The woman in a wheelchair at the potluck lunch,
whose glint in the eye
concealed a greater sickness,
was wheeled away in mid-conversation.
We never saw her again.

When my greatest love returns
after a short run of her errands,
it is for me the greatest relief,
a breath or two of joy,
  and a brighter eye sees her again.

There was a time when these
  comings and goings
  were taken for granted,
  a confidence perhaps
  that every departure surely meant
  a safe return.

But in that moment of deeply felt emotion,
    deeper than any belief or thought,
    when experience itself knows
    that coming into this human realm
    ensures with certainty that it will end,

    then the present becomes the folding in
    of past and future,
    the place where gratitude resides.

Working Toward a Simple Poem

Seemingly from the ether
the thought arose
first without words
then with words that jumbled into place:

There will come a time when I renounce
all that I have been saying, all that I have been writing.

The striving for an understanding that is satisfactory,
a knowing that arises from direct experience,
a transformation of the word *equanimous* from meaning to experience,
will displace the books of poetry
with a deepening
ever toward
something beyond current understanding,
something for which all the learning thus far
has been incapable of acquiring (or letting go),
to reveal the natural state
before all the barnacle-like impurities
accumulated, clinging like clams to a pier post.

Swimming so long in the pool of habit and delusion,
never having been introduced until late that others before
have examined closely the sources of ignorance,
I swim round and round, believing at times
that I may yet arrive at some destination that I, as yet,
do not recognize, but am certain that I will know it
when I see it.

I swim round and round in the brightest ideas
that have come my way by the brightest minds,
ricocheting from wall to wall in the deep end
and shallow end of the pool, absorbing and forgetting,

sometimes buoyant, sometimes sinking,
thrashing alone in the waters of a little pool.

Maybe when the swimmer admits to knowing nothing,
lets go of the striving to reach somewhere beyond the little pool,
and floats for a time without pretense of knowing the direction,
there will arise some hint or understanding.

With the patterns of habit so strong,
maybe the writing and questioning can continue
without attachment or urgency that some destination
must be reached.

There was a time when I thought
many, if not all, individuals examined life
as I do, but I see that this is not the case.
I see the strong appearances of happiness
in others, even with their pains and griefs.
Have they acquired the awareness and understanding
for which I am striving? I do not know.

All that I read from others
has been filtered,
even those words that appear raw and pained.
How close can language come to experience?

Even for those shared experiences
the words help us feel only our own experience.
A voice says again to stop the whirlybird words,
spinning round and round like maple seedlings.

Instead, there can be a poetry of display,
a kind of Sufi tale without analysis or punchline,
a wisdom tale or observation that is not proud of itself;
a modest and most often brief spreading of description

infused with a rare aromatic essence inseparable from
the carpet of description that is laid down
along the path of the poem.

In the wintry wood
where leaves and windswept twigs
settle softly on the forest floor,
each slow and cautious stepping foot
sends echoes to the nearby birds.

Touching the Twilight Realm

Some of the daytime dreams
   provided only glimpses,
   a brief decorative tableau,
   a miniature diorama photographed,
   a still life on the edge of provocation

   in need of movement
   like the old crank engines
   to get the dream car going.

Without warning, an image willed itself
   into being: a small group of people
   boarding or already seated
   on a tram, a concatenation
     of little enclosed cars
     on quiet rubber tires

   heading up the paved incline
   to the open underground cave.

Here the daydreamer drives the dream
   as the group walks through
   the lighted cave
   guided, informative, cordial;
   stopping here and there,
   stalactites, stalagmites,
   bat nests, water dripping,
   darkened corners, cold dampness,
   air moving through the cave
   deep underground.

A man stays behind as the group moves on;
   in an hour they exit the cave without the man
   and board the tram for the return ride.

The tram reaches the building where everyone
        gets off and walks to their cars,
        no one aware that the man
        is in the cave, alone in the dark.

The dreamer stays with the man all night
        sitting with eyes open in the pitch black darkness
        seated on a rock back in a corner
        dry and cool, listening to the silence
        and watching the darkness;
        only a distant slow dripping sound
        throughout the timeless night.

Now the dreamer is alone
        sitting in broad daylight
        on a park bench
        deep in the cave
        eyes fading shut toward a light doze
        rhythmic echoes, light heart pulsing
        like water dripping, or rain falling,
        the dreamer in daytime
        fading into the sidewalk spaces
        past the chalky hopscotch markings,
        pink hearts of love drawn on the sidewalk.

Drifting now into the weightless floating
        that always comes at this hour
        not even the distant motorcycle idling
        can pull him from this soft drifting slide
        toward the old haystacks at the end of summer days
        when the man was a child
        smelling the comfortable heat in the wheat
        and falling into the arms of loving family and friends,
        so many warm embraces before the spinning began
        and the running over tilled fields for help,
        screaming to anyone to come quickly

someone was hurt real bad
drifting again into the soft bumper cars
the small country fairs and the sticky cotton candy
the long drives through the desert,
stopping to see the two-headed snake
and the carved figures standing by the doorways
and the big boys in their jeans and white tee shirts
with their short sleeves rolled up
tucking in their hard cigarette packs.

And through the night the chill of the cave
      wakes the man or the dreamer on the bench,
      only to adjust an arm or leg before resuming
      the sleep that never ends.

The man in the cave or the dreamer sleeping in the park,
      or the man at home trying to make a living,
      staring deep into space,
      going somewhere with closed eyes in the light
      or open in the dark
      while everyone else walks by
      on their way to somewhere,
      no one calling out that someone is lost.

Nothing More Is Needed

These were moments of enchantment,
      sometimes musical, or simple breezes
      touching face and arms in sunlight
      while seated on a rock or log

Placid lakes ringed by pines and a floor of golden needles
      lake blue against needle greens and golden browns
        in morning's quiet stillness

When we lived with them, concentrating on nothing more,
      warm pine resin and salty seas in afternoon
        seen and heard and smelled,
        nothing more was needed

Before Sleep

The words had no intention of leaving,
    subvocal, euphonic, ceaseless repetition

    the cold sputtering engine
    of nonsense phrases
    jousted silently in the night

Arriving in the long minutes before sleep
    words arose, coalesced, tumbled forward
    contending with flames of meaning
    eventually to retreat like fading daffodils
    among the cold sheets of flower bed snow

All before adjusting the pillow
    the once sublime reaches of thought
    dropped their petals, disconsolate

    protuberant like other tubers
    pushing their way to flower
    in early sun-petaled spring

Words at first erupted into vignettes of imagination
    pushing their way toward somnolence
    eventually to lie in repose
    after some taming and tiring of mind

In the Old Peaceful Ways

In the old peaceful ways
we walked the hills
without worry that our words
     would be heard
     or remembered

We did not consider how our poems
     would be understood
     if they were read at all
     in a future so different
          from our time

Our dreams, too, were different
     in their softness
     when sleep was welcomed
        and given time
        to ripen into windows
        of mystery and new understanding

We closed our eyes in the quiet darkness
     safe and warm and dry
     and if we had seen meteor showers
     or the bright full moon, we saw them again
        with closed eyes before sleeping

Before sleeping we saw again the pines
     and cypress, the royal maples,
     and the sprawling berry vines
     and the winding paths we had walked

And though we gave little thought to the future
     of dreams and remembrances

we wrote them down or spoke of them
as if they had some greater meaning
       beyond our own present time

And in that time of precious wanderings
       we met other travelers
       who shared similar paths and dreams,
       and in that time it was comforting to know
              we were not alone

What We Slept Through

How far we have come

Not only in the traveling,
        mostly on foot or riding
        on one animal or another,
        being pulled by a swaying cart

But also in the pauses and rests
        that lasted many generations
        in valley communities
        so often near fresh flowing water

And our families stayed long enough
        around lakes to learn the ways
        of water and ice

        eventually to learn the richness
        of river-bottom soils
        and to plant the best saved seeds

We saved our strength and slept:
        we dreamed of fiery phantoms
        slept inside animal skins
        took on their spirits
        slept through the separation
            of continents
            and the mile-deep ice sheets
        we slept through the pestilence
            all around us
        and in that sleeping we dreamed

A recurring dream invaded our waking life,
broke through the doors and took residence
refusing to remain bottled in sleep

In the dream that hijacked the living daylight,
our eyes commanded us to separate ourselves
from all that entered their apertures

The ears too heard what was out there
as separate from something we called we
      behind the scales of our body armor

The nose and mouth and skin had their
      complementary sensory inputs,
        their own armaments to seal off self from
      not-self

And the waking brain dreamed its phantasms
so tightly that we dreamed day and night
through the drifting of continents
like little boats blown to sea
and we dreamed up the I
separate and alien
giving birth to the conqueror,
to fear and dissatisfaction
and all that we live with
      in this separation

The dream today is the tunnel space
      we go to
      we crawl through

to the open space dissolution of our assumptions

and we return from the tunnel space
to record our journeys

between two worlds:
a living dream world of appearances and illusion
and a world that is beyond our knowing or experience

how we long for liberation
from the known confinements and defilements
in exchange for the understanding of a truth
          we do not experience

The mind is the way station
          the crawl space between known illusion
          and the unknown real that we abandoned
          in our long dreaming sleep

No longer do we know where the illusion lies

And so in these nights of dreaming
          past the riches of our acquisitions
          we seek beyond the human realm
          and the drifting continents that brought us here
          to discover what it is we will be waking to
                    if we waken at all

Part III: Toward the Waking State

In the Stillness and Silence

For a long time
the dreams did not appear,
or they came in strange fragments,
phantoms of the mind
thrown before the sleeping eyes,
like ejecta littering the landscape,
unglittering pumice;
nothing of note to suggest meaning or connection
in the sameness of our days.

In the all-too-familiar nightness of being,
we searched for onyx and obsidian,
something of importance in the unusual,
something at least shiny to the eye and smooth to the touch,
within the otherwise grayness and blackness
of this volcanic lunar landscape.

It did not occur to us then
that the stillness of the place was the gem
we had been searching for,
and that the silence all around us
that we had been clambering to avoid
would be our teacher.

We were like astronauts far from home
or wanderers in a lavaland that seemed endless
in duration, and unchanging to our insensitive eyes.

We had seen and endured the sadnesses
of earthquake and war alike,
the carnage and rubble
sweeping away lifetimes of collected moments,
friends and family disappeared in a violent instant,
some never recovered

except in tortured memories
and through tears that weighed down on hearts,
some never to mend.

Behind the parapets of privileged safety
we had learned to sit,
and out of our quiet contemplation
we came upon the teachings of others,
the wisest who came before us,
observing the sources of dissatisfaction and pain,
the consequences of clinging and aversion;
the quiet glimpses that the world of appearances
contained within it the possibilities for deeper understanding:
two worlds existing within each other.

Those discoveries we made long ago
in times of comfort, before the darkening of skies
and the leveling of landscapes.

Now we carry our understanding
like jewels in a basket
through the unfamiliar days that are often
enshrouded in smoke blotting the sun's light
and choking out the pathways to life.

We seat ourselves on a fearful precipice,
not even a tree to lean against through the night,
where the warm updrafts provide a brief respite
from the sooty and stagnant stillness,
and looking out upon the lifeless appearance
of smoldering rubble and sharp rocky shapes,
we remove the shawl of selfhood,
let go of seeing and hearing,
tasting and smelling,
and all bodily and mental sensations,
and with them the cloak of "I"

slips free into a realm beyond reflection,
the final gift of gratitude
for having glimpsed the formations
that brought us to this understanding,
a kind of awakening.

Glaucoma Visionaries

The stars were visible
only at the periphery of our vision.
How many other sideways glances, we wondered,
provided our only way of seeing?

How much else in our travels
was out of view when we looked directly at them?
Those signs about flooded roads ahead;
the people running straight for us
        with hands waving above their heads;
        the rising water at our feet.

Was it our blindness that pulled us forward,
        or a kind of ignorance of the impediments
            strewn across our path?
We were dreamers swimming upstream
        against a current that pulled at our flanks.
The winds whispered their warnings
        that we did not heed
        in our refusal to believe
        that storms could catch us.

And somehow we pushed on, traveling with the sun
        at our back, musing that some understanding
        awaited our arrival around an unknown corner,
            if only we persisted.

At times the labyrinthine switchbacks were dizzying,
        corkscrews through the mountains
        and endless boggy waterways.

At night the nebulae swirled above our heads
        in the clear desert skies,
        the brighter stars always at the outer edges.

And in the morning, we wiped the whimsical webs
        from our eyes and from the windshield
        of our house on wheels before driving away,
        confident that our peripheral glimpses
        would carry us through another day.

One Glimpse

Between birth and death
the one chance;

like eye opening
to see the way light comes in,

to feel the flow of water
on its downward motive course;

the effortless furling and patterned swirls
of plants and riverbeds;

opportunities at every stage
for acceptance of the way

to live in accord
with what is given,

with the way
effect follows cause
like shadows follow the walking legs

or the skip-rope jitter-bug move
across the dance floor
of day after day breakout
from the day before
and all the ways
music moved in the past.

Both hands waving above the head,
feet lilting and shifting soft and smooth
bringing in the sun and moonlight,
listening to the smoky jazz through the open doors,
smiling miles a minute, coasting on the old sounds

saying "so what" with horn and sax
through the blue notes of the night.

We fall on our backs
and look to the stars
forgetting for the moment
where we were going
and who we are;

the privileged ones
given the big frontal cortex
to see beyond the slow burn
of the entertained mind;

to look to those stars with awe
and no wish to conquer and exploit;
to look to our origins
and the origins of our delusions
of who we are;

So we lie there in the sand,
ocean waves cooling our feet
on the inflow of tide,
no care for the moment;
the cares can wait for this moment
listening to the song of the sea

We ride the windy glimpse,
feeling the pulse of the earth
in the rhythm of our steps;
in the sway of the hips;
in the side glances
to see who is sharing our dancing beat.

And in the sun's glare
while the warmth relaxes the bones,

we remind ourselves
what a time to be alive;
what a time to catch ourselves
looking back from all the views in space,
grateful to be granted this moment
right here
right now.

In a Land of Plenty

As a practical matter
       debilitation reigned.
       Cities were sacked
       on the fifteen-yard line.

The causeway to the City of Light
       lay in ruins on the drafting table.
       No work was completed for the populus
       the whole day long.

Laughter and cackling filled the air;
       bears and half-naked men
       filled the stadium
       and from afar
       the loud and slurred amusements
       concealed a world of pain.

In the tenements next door to daylong laughter and gaiety
       thin and tenebrous lives
       toiled in the filtered light, seeking the finest strands
       and thinnest fibers through the glass-less windows,
       as a nickels-worth of water
       dripped through the clogged pipes
       into flat saucers for the parched lips
       that waited all day to lick the plates.

Waiters in wealthy mansions slid a thumb-sized morsel from a plate
       or licked a gravy-stained finger
       on the way back to the kitchen;
       the rich and wealthy siphoned their own portions
       from their offices in broad daylight.

And in ancient Rome the lava bubbled beneath the well-traveled streets
       where fissures and vents hissed loudly through the night.

Seeds of Gratitude

Trained by the the urban expectations
       of easy water and food

and raised in safety and protection
       from threats that we did not know of

enshrouded in a fog that prevented
       us from seeing the world

       as it was
       and would become

we took our first steps outward
       still tied to the umbilical
       of nearness and comfort
       to encounter our first unscripted days

The voice that stayed with us said:
"Let us be grateful for the people, plants, and animals
       that have contributed to this meal or helped
       to ease our travels from place to place"

       without destination except to learn
       and cast off illusions that still cling
       from a life that molded us into stone

All around us we hear the voices of bitterness and hate,
and still we travel with gratitude among the kindest of hearts
who share their talents and kindness.

Two worlds overlapping, one like a barking dog tethered to a post;
       the other a warm soft breeze, fragrant, non-demanding,
       like a welcoming reminder from around some corner in the past

We leave one and then another
>with a pat on the shoulder
>a look in the eye, and a thank you
>from the heart

>and that is enough
>one at a time
>the seeds of gratitude received, shared, and planted.

Mother, Father, Sister

They have gone
this time forever
out of reach
        and beyond any calls

and still this sense of waiting

to share some news
little milestones
a closeness expressed
in morsels
so imaginatively small

we never thought about endings
when we had all the time
        in the world

sometimes wondering
what conversations we would have had
if we had a chance today
        knowing what we now know
        about death's insistent turn

and now untethered
in a kind of orphaned freedom
these unanswered calls
on days of remembrance
        are woven into the day
        like the cold November wind
        announcing another winter

We Who Rest in Healing Waters

Sitting in one of the four outdoor tubs
      amid the quiet talking of others
      in hot mineral water
      flowing in, draining out

In the welcoming relaxation, the first calmness
      in months, the skin opened up
      like the doors of prison,
      like the floodgates of hell

Out poured first the pain of the day's exertions
      through dry desert hills;
      then out came the body's oils
      carrying toxins long held
      in the brittle joints and bending parts;

In a convulsion of tears
out flowed memories faster than I could recall
like tiny monstrous bats racing at my face in the night;
the past traumas came in through the locked doors
and more tears fell from my face into the hot mineral water
enshrouding me, pulling out debris that had remained sealed
      inside for years, for decades, for this long tiring lifetime.

The first untended griefs bounded out
      in pulsing flashes of long-forgotten images
      mother, father, sister
      accompanied by deep feelings of regret
      a spasm of twitching muscles,
      uncontrolled sorrowful shaking of limbs and torso.

The deepest tissues, tightened for years,
      leaving me bent and stooped,
      began to unwind

in rapid electrical short circuiting,
firing hot bursts of pain inside and outside my head.

A constellation of nerve pain
        atop my head
        cascaded over my face
        to pulsate and crawl for months.
        What lessons will I learn
        when the writhing ends
        in these heated healing waters?

Then unbeckoned, the first forgotten memory surfaced calmly
        from the hot mineral water:

Beth was a smart and serious student in eighth grade;
the only blind person I had ever known in school.
One day she asked if she could feel my face
to get a mental sense of its shape and structure;
the light staccato tapping of her sensitive moist fingers
moved slowly over my forehead, jaws, nose, and lips.
She held my face in her warm caring hands,
        unashamed of this intimacy
        she felt my acceptance.

Her intense concentration traced the contours of my face,
        She gathered insight in her fingertips
        while I looked into those dark sunken and unseeing eyes
        sealed forever from the light and colors
        that have accompanied all my days since birth.

Sinking deeper into the embrace of the healing waters,
        the boundaries of skin and water dissolved,
        my limbs and torso floated away from feeling
        as my slow-bobbing head held all my body's sensations,
        gently floating while the movement of water flowed
        into and out of the large tub in the desert sun.

Inside my ears the lub dub pulsing of my heart,
      the familiar rhythm that accompanied me before birth,
      my mother's heart beating life into the wrinkles
          and folds of this early body.

From the aqueous pulsations, more memories emerged.
      I am ten years old, standing with father and grandfather
      on the short wooden pier on Colpoy's Bay,
      fishing poles in our hands,
      fifteen years before grandfather's leg amputation,
      deep blue lake and sky.
      The older father and son on good behavior
      almost 30 years after son left home.
      So many unanswered questions.
      All gone now, only the photo of memory.

The time comes to leave the healing waters,
      to step back into the wind,
      the commotion of the middle world
      that this wrinkling body inhabits,
      to see with these wondrous and grateful eyes
      the contours and patterns of the landscapes before me.

Settling into the calmness
of this fortunate life
where pain and soothing waters entwine,
      almost conspire,
      to bring me to another precipice
      to share what these eyes do see
      and to rest finally, accepting the changes,
         and to marvel
         at what comes and goes,
         including this mirage
         that is me.

Trees

Some trees grow taller than others,
>   spreading leaf-covered branches wide
>   into open spaces toward sunlight,
>   their trunks strong, straight, and solid.

Others grow toward the light from the shadows
>   of the canopy, their narrow branches bending
>   and twisting each year, their trunks still
>   the food of deer in their upward turn.

The strong and the weak alike
>   shed their leaves and needles
>   each autumn into winter,
>   lay down their bark and trunks
>   in time, becoming once again
>   food for another cycle.

We're All Tourists Just Passing Through

Two young women approached us,
each holding a dog on a leash
sunny warm afternoon, Florida bay in the background.
One of the dogs immediately came to me
       as I knelt on a knee;

With its muzzle near my mouth,
       not to lick, but to smell and sniff.
       And before the woman could ask
       if I had recently eaten a lunch,
       I thought of the cancer-sensitive dogs
       who needed only to smell one's breath.
       Could this be one of them?
       An early warning? A confirmation of
       what I have been denying.

We walked on and a muted sunset followed.

Breathing in a long breath
       I know I am breathing in a long breath
Breathing out a long breath
       I am aware it's a long breath I am breathing out

The dog's moist nose was inches from my mouth
       its green eyes looking into mine
I broke off the relationship lest it curl at my feet,
       a devoted and knowing caregiver for life,
       communicating without language.

Very calm, very tranquil
       attention rests at the place outside the nostrils
       where the breath cuts,
       feel the whole body inside
       feel the whole body outside.

In a moment of distraction
        the thought runs to
        a cove in Kauai
        where we scooped white shells
        from below our feet in the clear blue water.
        These curving shells had been the homes
        of living creatures long ago,
        and there was no end to their numbers
        ebbing and flowing with the tides beneath our feet.

Another observation, whether distraction or insight,
        a recollection seeing homes passed on our travels,
        from gated palm-lined communities
        to bundles of blankets and cardboard
        piled beneath concrete overpasses,
        someone's dwelling for a time.

Like the shells and homes that have their day,
the breath moves in and out
arising and passing away
impurities removed,

even the devotion of the caregiver
moving from moment to moment
has its warm afternoon
        before sunset.

The House at the Edge of Town

When we bought the house
we did not know
that it was supported
on the backs of turtles
all the way down.

Several doors led into the house,
so many ways to enter,
with windows two on each side
like eyes peering out of a protected skull.

From the curlicued apertures in the attic
we listened to all the sounds
that reached us from town,
including voices from the sidewalk
and leaves tapping on the gutters.

We tasted the snow and storms
from the gaping mouth of the front porch,
and smelled the changing seasons
from its swinging cushioned chairs.

The walls all the way around
felt the vibrations from outdoors,
including the heat of summer
and cold of winter, and the pressure of storms,
like the sensitive nerves of a body.

The living room was the place of thinking,
where we gathered to share our sorrows,
generate reminiscence and formulate plans,
to bring together the sense of a whole
and perceptions of our continuing existence.

We have lived long in this house,
getting comfortable with the neighbors
whose houses appear like our own.
And now the word enters
from out of our long questioning
bearing news of a great illusion
born of ignorance.

When we sit beneath a tree
on the adjacent hillside
looking toward our house,
we see that the porch is not the house,
nor the windows or the doors;
We see that the living room
is not separate or unchanging.
What seemed unified and lasting
arises and falls away
in lessons of impermanence.

And we know that this knowing
does not prevent us from
inhabiting this house or interacting again and again
with the neighbors and the impermanent world
all around us.

And we know that this knowing
will not rest or go away.
In our living room we contemplate
with every subtle thought
the limitations of our thinking
as we seek an understanding
of the more deeply real
when all that we have known
is peeled away.

In our unwillingness to abandon our house
we are caught in our constant striving
walking at the edge of one world
while taking slow steps toward entering the stream
across the way, immersing ourselves peacefully
beyond our world of illusion.

We are not dwelling in two worlds,
but feeling the disenchantment
that invites us to be open to possibilities
to examine our experiences
with a wisdom that emerges only
in the extremity of an open willingness.

In this world of appearances, the warm sun
casts its golden orange glow
against the leafless west-facing trees
on the distant hillside,
and out from this house
there emanates a gratitude
that arises with the sun's golden glow.

A Moment in Destin, Florida

Today we walked on a crushed granite beach,
fine sugar-white sand holding back the sea
tiny scalloped shells
fit for souvenir earrings
at our feet

a day where anything could have happened
in the world we left behind
and we wouldn't have known of it

but it is an insistent world
that waits for our return
to pull us in like a rip tide.

The long pier above in the distance
reaches into the Gulf
inviting strollers to stand above the waters
for a time.

If you walk too far out
you may not get back.
The yellow flags offer caution
to adventurers who might step
into the emerald deep-turning waves.

This is the edge of the world,
so we must circle back,
follow these sandy lands
past the pines and palms
into the interior forests
until they too reach their limits
and we enter southwestern deserts

where days are longer and skies higher,
leading us into the warm dry wooded north
where again we rejuvenate our sojourning hearts,
finding a world that lies always at our feet.

M Is for Love

Somewhere above this sublunary miasma
blue bejeweled Betelgeuse,
like wedding ring in the night sky,
        spins

conch shells spin too,
as does the old curled white pine
used for carving canes

and the sperm of whales and hominins
boring their way with pigtails swimming

cutting their way like rivers to the sea
leaving their curved and carved imprints
in the sandy waterswept inlets

rarely in a straight line
does water flow,
its course wandering
with the easy curves

this is the watercourse way
the way of galaxies
and the tendrils of bean and fern,
climbing and swirling toward
the open spaces.

And so with the old man bent forward,
lost in thought, looking for shells
or wandering in curving swirls on the sandy shore,
the first reflections of stars
through the watery pools in his eyes,
curved fingers gripping a cane,
fading memories swirling

in fragments and filaments
spinning loose into galaxies of thought,
heading toward the easy places,
gazing out to sea or inward
toward some sanctuary of retreat.

And in the gloaming
on the same sandy shore
he sees first an apparition before him
then the half familiar form
and the growing comfort he calls love,
he knows she is here to save him again
she is walking toward him
bringing a handful of shells
her smile and a warm curving hand
fingers now interlaced in his
guiding him along the easy shore
back to the home he had been looking for.

Mid-Morning Musings in a Wood

While we hacked into the bark
     of the tree
starry-eyed seekers of the heartwood
     knowing nothing
peeling away bark to stare at the whitewood
     of the girdled tree
     soon to dry and die in the sun

even the libraries of Alexandria
     would bring us no closer to knowing

We built rafts from all the dead trees
     we had gathered and pillaged
     to navigate across the inviting waters

At first we brought our books of learning
     and they, too, sunk to the water's depths
     from the capsized rafts

We knew nothing then, as we know nothing now
     training our minds by observing others

We burned the soles of our feet on pilgrimages
     seeking the wisdom of the heartwood

Learned to eat our morning gruel and nothing more
     even trying later to live on nettle soup
     all to no avail

We traded our work clothes and belts for robes and loin cloths
     sitting in the snow
     getting no closer to the heartwood

Along the way we kept hearing teachers say
        "Do not rely on thinking your way to heartwood"
        too much thinking

In the deepest waters we began sinking
        at first grabbing on
        then letting go
        somehow floating on,
        guided perhaps to what awaits

Now we travel safely on land
        our axes put away
        eating our gruel with contentment
        not too much of this world or the next
        cultivating gratitude in slow and even measure
        without expectation of breakthroughs around the bend
        or headlight beams guiding the way

        standing nearer to the trees
        our feet planted firmly on the ground
        looking less starry eyed in our growing patience
        content for now in the heart of this wooded grove

Toward Being

Early on, the concepts,
            theories,
                        speculations,

the analysis of inner and outer worlds
elaborated into labyrinths of meaning
        entrapped by the perspective
        that enough knowledge
                will bear fruit
                like happiness or power
                        or insight.

At times, knowledge reaches the intersection
        of understanding impermanence, entropy

                even the complex living forms
                    break down,
                    return again to the elemental.

And so too the poetry of effort
        relaxes its grip;
        seeing there is nothing to teach,
                no need for deep abstraction,
                no ultimate destination.

The new practice becomes a yielding
        to the glimpses
        of wise old simplicity.

The ancients knew this—
setting down the description, stepping aside,
being present in the observation;

no longer interpreting meanings and signs;
patient, attentive, and grateful.

Seeing the petrified log today—
wood now stone;
that, too, is how it goes.

Tonight the wind groans,
         rocking our house on wheels,
         warm stillness inside.

Going forward, time to cultivate a new practice of being
         with water
                  rock
                     time.

Awakening from Long Sleep

During the long sleep
      we dreamed

We dreamed at first
      of manicured orchards in bloom
      and cloudless skies placed there
      for our own pleasure

For our own pleasures and amusements
      we dreamed

We dreamed of ease and comfort
      we dreamed of freedom for all
      when we dreamed beyond ourselves

When we sought the pleasures for ourselves
it blinded us from the suffering of our neighbors
      here and everywhere

And from our dreams we began to hear the refrain
      that it was time to awaken
      that it was long past time to awaken
      there was work to be done

For so long we dreamed on, harboring
      the old habits of comfort
      before the songs of resistance arrived

And out of our dreaming at long last
      the smallest seed was sown,
      the long-germinating humming and groaning
      and we began seeking a way forward

In the sweet rhythms we heard the calls
        of freedom songs
        calling us forward,
        time to rise up they sang
        in their soft insistence

Toward the sweet rhythms we climbed
        out of our dreamy sleep and slumber
        taking the first earnest steps forward

We had wandered long toward the precipice
        where the waking twilight realm
        meets the advancing night of dreams

And we knew, at last, that it was time
        to waken from the dreams
        that had guided us toward
        the blinding depths of unreason

Dante's infernal rings would have shaken us
        ever more quickly into the wakened state,
        but we had no such fears and flames
        in our dreamlike slumber

We took, instead, the long march
        not even knowing
        that we were on a path
                or on a treadmill

We were guided by the choices we made,
        each turn with its own consequence,
        and not until we examined finally
        the conditions that brought us here
        did we admit that a crisis had arrived

The need to awaken was the natural urging
       that brought us forward willingly
       out of the twilight realm

And from this vantage point we peer into new spaces,
       another place for open-eyed poems
       where music of the heart
       waits for a further unfolding

About the Author

Don Langford is the author of *In the Light of the Full Moon: Dispersions, Glimpses, and Reflections* and *Songs from Deep Time*. He writes and travels full time with his wife, Marlene. His forthcoming poetry collection is entitled *Water Rock Time*.